I0820079

30
Minutes
OR LESS
RECIPES

pil
Publications International, Ltd.

Louis Weber, CEO
Publications International, Ltd.
8140 Lehigh Ave
Morton Grove, IL 60053

Pictured on the front cover *(clockwise from top left):* Smashed Burgers *(page 116),* Classic Turkey Tacos *(page 106),* Greek Salad Bowl *(page 96),* Quinoa Chili *(page 81),* Creamy Macaroni and Broccoli *(page 74),* Steak Fajitas *(page 164),* Puttanesca Pasta *(page 64)* and Mongolian Beef *(page 6).*

Pictured on the back cover *(left to right):* Crunchy Kale Salad *(page 172),* Orecchiette with Sausage and Broccoli Rabe *(page 56)* and Cajun Rice *(page 88).*

ISBN: 978-1-63938-880-6

Manufactured in China.

8 7 6 5 4 3 2 1

Microwave Cooking: Microwave ovens vary in wattage. Use the cooking times as guidelines and check for doneness before adding more time.

Let's get social!

@Publications_International

@PublicationsInternational

www.pilbooks.com

Contents

Main Meats & Fish

Maple and Sage Pork Chops

MAKES 4 SERVINGS

- 2 tablespoons finely chopped fresh sage
- 2 teaspoons olive oil
- ½ teaspoon salt
- 4 boneless pork chops (about 4 ounces each)
- 2 teaspoons maple syrup

1 Preheat broiler. Combine sage, oil and salt in small bowl. Rub mixture evenly over pork chops. Place on baking sheet.

2 Broil pork chops 4 minutes. Turn over; brush evenly with syrup. Broil 4 minutes or until pork chops are browned and barely pink in center (145°F).

Mongolian Beef

MAKES 4 SERVINGS

- 1 cup uncooked rice
- 1¼ pounds beef flank steak
- ¼ cup cornstarch
- 3 tablespoons vegetable oil, divided
- 3 cloves garlic, minced
- 2 teaspoons grated fresh ginger
- ½ cup water
- ½ cup soy sauce
- ⅓ cup packed dark brown sugar
- Pinch red pepper flakes
- 2 green onions, diagonally sliced into 1-inch pieces

1 Cook rice according to package directions.

2 Meanwhile, cut flank steak in half lengthwise, then cut crosswise (against the grain) into ¼-inch slices. Combine beef and cornstarch in medium bowl; toss to coat.

3 Heat 1 tablespoon oil in large skillet or wok over high heat. Add half of beef in single layer (do not crowd); cook 1 to 2 minutes per side or until browned. Remove to clean bowl. Repeat with remaining beef and 1 tablespoon oil.

4 Heat remaining 1 tablespoon oil in same skillet over medium heat. Add garlic and ginger; cook and stir 30 seconds. Add water, soy sauce, brown sugar and red pepper flakes; bring to a boil, stirring until well blended. Cook 8 minutes or until sauce is slightly thickened, stirring occasionally.

5 Return beef to skillet; cook 2 to 3 minutes or until sauce thickens and beef is heated through. Stir in green onions. Serve over rice.

Balsamic-Glazed Sirloin and Spinach

MAKES 4 SERVINGS

- **5 tablespoons olive oil, divided**
- **2 Vidalia or other sweet onions, thinly sliced**
- **3 tablespoons balsamic vinegar, divided**
- **1¼ teaspoons salt, divided**
- **1 teaspoon coarsely ground black pepper**
- **1 pound top sirloin steak (1 inch thick)**
- **1 package (about 10 ounces) fresh spinach, coarsely chopped**

1 Heat 2 tablespoons oil in large skillet over medium-high heat. Add onions; cook 10 minutes or until softened, stirring occasionally. Sprinkle with 1 tablespoon vinegar and ½ teaspoon salt; cook 10 minutes or until beginning to brown, stirring occasionally.

2 Meanwhile, press pepper onto both sides of steak. Rub with ½ teaspoon vinegar; sprinkle with ½ teaspoon salt. Heat 1 tablespoon oil in another large skillet over medium-high heat. Add steak; cook 5 minutes. Turn and cook 3 to 5 minutes more for medium rare (135°F) or to desired doneness. Transfer steak to cutting board; tent with foil. Let stand 5 minutes before slicing.

3 Add remaining 2 tablespoons oil to skillet. Add spinach; cover and cook 2 minutes. Stir spinach; cook 1 minute if necessary to wilt all of spinach. Add remaining vinegar and ¼ teaspoon salt; cook and stir 1 minute.

4 Cut steak into thin slices; serve over spinach and onions.

Sesame Chicken

MAKES 4 SERVINGS

- **1 pound boneless skinless chicken breasts or thighs, cut into 1-inch pieces**
- **⅔ cup teriyaki sauce, divided**
- **Sweet and Sour Noodles (recipe follows) or hot cooked rice (optional)**
- **2 teaspoons cornstarch**
- **1 tablespoon peanut or vegetable oil**
- **2 cloves garlic, minced**
- **2 green onions, cut into ½-inch slices**
- **1 tablespoon sesame seeds, toasted***
- **1 teaspoon toasted sesame oil**

***To toast sesame seeds, cook and stir in small skillet over medium-low heat 3 minutes or until seeds begin to pop and turn golden.**

1. Combine chicken and ⅓ cup teriyaki sauce in medium bowl; toss to coat. Marinate in refrigerator 15 to 20 minutes. Meanwhile, prepare Sweet and Sour Noodles, if desired.
2. Drain chicken; discard marinade. Stir remaining ⅓ cup teriyaki sauce into cornstarch in small bowl until smooth.
3. Heat peanut oil in wok or large skillet over medium-high heat. Add chicken and garlic; stir-fry 3 minutes or until chicken is cooked through (165°F) and no longer pink in center. Stir cornstarch mixture; add to wok. Cook and stir 1 minute or until sauce boils and thickens. Stir in green onions, sesame seeds and sesame oil. Serve with noodles.

Sweet and Sour Noodles

Combine ¼ cup teriyaki sauce, 3 tablespoons rice vinegar, 3 cloves garlic, minced, 1 tablespoon toasted sesame oil and ¼ teaspoon chili oil, if desired, in large bowl. Cook 1 package (10 ounces) dried lo mein noodles according to package directions. Drain and place in bowl with sauce; mix well. Stir in 1 cup sliced red bell pepper and 3 sliced green onions.

Pork Chops with Vinegar Peppers

MAKES 4 SERVINGS

- 4 pork chops (about 1 inch thick)
- ½ teaspoon salt
- ¼ teaspoon black pepper
- 2 tablespoons olive oil
- 1½ cups seeded hot cherry peppers, cut into ½-inch slices*
- 2 cloves garlic, minced
- ¼ cup liquid from cherry pepper jar
- ¼ cup water
- 1 sprig fresh rosemary

***Hot cherry peppers are also available presliced in rings.**

1. Season both sides of pork with salt and black pepper.
2. Heat oil in large skillet over medium-high heat. Add pork chops; cook about 5 minutes per side or until browned. Remove to plate; keep warm.
3. Add cherry peppers and garlic to skillet; cook and stir 2 minutes over medium heat, scraping up browned bits from bottom of skillet. Stir in cherry pepper liquid, water and rosemary.
4. Return pork chops along with any accumulated juices to skillet; cover and cook about 6 minutes or until pork is barely pink in center (145°F).

Meat Loaf Patties with Skillet Rice

MAKES 4 SERVINGS

- 12 ounces ground beef
- 4 ounces bulk pork or turkey sausage
- ⅔ cup picante sauce, divided
- 2 eggs
- ½ cup quick or old-fashioned oats
- 1 tablespoon vegetable oil
- 2 tablespoons ketchup
- 1 teaspoon Worcestershire sauce
- 1 cup uncooked instant brown rice
- ½ cup water

1. Combine beef, sausage, ⅓ cup picante sauce, eggs and oats in medium bowl. Shape into four ½-inch-thick patties. Heat oil in large nonstick skillet over medium heat. Add patties; cook 5 minutes.
2. Meanwhile, combine 2 tablespoons picante sauce, ketchup and Worcestershire sauce in small bowl. Turn patties. Spoon 1 tablespoon picante mixture on each patty. Reduce heat to medium-low; cover and cook 10 to 12 minutes or until no longer pink in centers (160°F).
3. Meanwhile, cook rice according to package directions.
4. Remove patties to plate. Add water, remaining picante sauce and rice to skillet; stir to scrape up browned bits. Place patties on rice mixture; simmer 3 minutes.

Chicken with Garlic Sauce

MAKES 4 SERVINGS

- 1 cup uncooked rice
- 4 boneless skinless chicken breasts (about 6 ounces each)
- ¾ teaspoon salt, divided
- ½ teaspoon black pepper, divided
- ¼ cup plus 1 tablespoon olive oil, divided
- ¼ cup all-purpose flour
- 1½ cups thinly sliced onions
- 1 green bell pepper, sliced
- 4 cloves garlic, minced
- 1 can (about 14 ounces) chicken broth

1. Cook rice according to package directions.
2. Meanwhile, season chicken with ¼ teaspoon salt and ¼ teaspoon pepper. Heat 1 tablespoon oil in large skillet over medium-high heat. Add chicken; cook on one side 2 minutes or until browned. Transfer chicken to plate.
3. Reduce heat to medium. Add flour and remaining ¼ cup oil to skillet; cook and stir 3 minutes or until flour begins to brown. Add green onions, bell pepper and garlic; cook and stir 5 minutes or until onions are translucent.
4. Add broth and remaining ½ teaspoon salt and ¼ teaspoon pepper; stir until smooth. Bring to a boil, stirring occasionally. Add chicken, browned side up, and any accumulated juices; return to a boil. Reduce heat to low; cover and simmer 15 to 20 minutes or until chicken is cooked through (165°F) and no longer pink in center. Serve over rice.

Taco-Topped Potatoes

MAKES 4 SERVINGS

- 4 russet potatoes (8 to 12 ounces each), scrubbed and pierced with fork
- 8 ounces ground beef
- ½ (1¼-ounce) package taco seasoning mix
- ½ cup water
- 1 cup diced tomatoes
- ¼ teaspoon salt
- 2 cups shredded lettuce
- ½ cup (2 ounces) shredded Cheddar cheese
- ¼ cup chopped green onions
- ½ cup sour cream

1. Microwave potatoes on HIGH 6 to 7 minutes or until fork-tender.
2. Brown beef in large skillet over medium-high heat 6 to 8 minutes, stirring to break up meat. Drain fat. Stir in seasoning mix and water. Reduce heat to low; simmer 5 minutes, stirring occasionally.
3. Combine tomatoes and salt in medium bowl.
4. Split potatoes almost in half and fluff with fork. Fill with beef mixture, tomatoes, lettuce, cheese and green onions. Serve with sour cream.

Pork Scaloppine

MAKES 4 TO 6 SERVINGS

- ⅓ cup all-purpose flour
- ¾ teaspoon salt
- ½ teaspoon black pepper
- 1 pound pork tenderloin, cut into ½-inch-thick slices
- 3 tablespoons olive oil, divided
- 1 package (16 ounces) sliced mushrooms
- ½ cup sliced green onions
- ½ cup water
- ¼ cup dry white wine
- ½ teaspoon dried marjoram
- ½ teaspoon dried basil
- ½ cup chopped pimiento-stuffed green olives (optional)
- Hot cooked orzo or rice

1 Combine flour, salt and pepper in shallow bowl. Pound pork slices to ¼-inch thickness between two sheets of plastic wrap with meat mallet or rolling pin. Coat each slice with flour mixture, shaking off excess.

2 Heat 1 tablespoon oil in large skillet over medium-high heat. Add mushrooms; cook and stir 6 to 8 minutes or until tender, stirring occasionally. Transfer to medium bowl; keep warm.

3 Heat remaining 2 tablespoons oil in same skillet. Add pork; cook 1 to 2 minutes per side or until browned. Add green onions, water, wine, marjoram and basil; bring to a simmer. Stir in olives, if desired. Cover and cook 6 to 8 minutes or until pork is barely pink in center (145°F), turning slices once. Remove pork to serving platter.

4 Return mushrooms to skillet; cook 2 to 3 minutes or until heated through. Serve pork with sauce and orzo.

Chicken Balinese

MAKES 4 SERVINGS

- 1 cup uncooked rice
- 8 boneless skinless chicken thighs
- ¼ teaspoon salt
- ¼ teaspoon black pepper
- 1 small onion, chopped
- 8 roasted cashews
- 2 cloves garlic
- 1 tablespoon chopped fresh ginger
- ¼ teaspoon ground red pepper
- 2 tablespoons vegetable oil
- ½ cup ketchup
- 1 tablespoon packed brown sugar
- 1 tablespoon soy sauce
- Lime wedges (optional)

1. Cook rice according to package directions.
2. Meanwhile, cut chicken crosswise into ¾-inch-wide strips. Place on large plate; sprinkle with salt and pepper.
3. Combine onion, cashews, garlic, ginger and red pepper in food processor or blender; process until smooth paste forms. Set aside.
4. Heat wok over medium-high heat 1 minute or until hot. Drizzle oil into wok and heat 30 seconds. Add chicken; stir-fry about 4 minutes or until chicken is cooked through (165°F) and no longer pink in center. Reduce heat to medium.
5. Add onion mixture to wok; stir-fry 2 minutes. Add ketchup, brown sugar and soy sauce; cook and stir until sugar dissolves and chicken is coated. Serve chicken with rice and lime wedges, if desired.

Stir-Fried Beef and Spinach

MAKES 2 SERVINGS

- 2 tablespoons vegetable oil, divided
- 1 package (6 ounces) fresh spinach, stemmed and torn
- 8 ounces boneless beef top sirloin steak, thinly sliced
- ¼ cup stir-fry sauce
- 1 teaspoon sugar
- ½ teaspoon curry powder
- ¼ teaspoon ground ginger

1. Heat 1 tablespoon oil in large skillet or wok over high heat. Add spinach; cook and stir 1 minute or until wilted. Transfer spinach to serving platter; keep warm.
2. Heat remaining 1 tablespoon oil in same skillet over high heat. Add beef; cook and stir 2 minutes or until barely pink. Add stir-fry sauce, sugar, curry powder and ginger; cook and stir 1½ minutes or until sauce thickens. Serve with spinach.

Quick and Easy Sautéed Chicken

MAKES 4 SERVINGS

- 4 boneless skinless chicken breasts (about 6 ounces each)
- 1 teaspoon smoked or regular paprika
- 1 teaspoon dried thyme
- ½ teaspoon garlic salt
- ⅛ teaspoon ground red pepper
- 2 teaspoons olive oil

1 Place chicken between sheets of waxed paper or plastic wrap; pound to even ½-inch thickness. Combine paprika, thyme, garlic salt and red pepper in small bowl; rub over both sides of chicken.

2 Heat oil in large nonstick skillet over medium heat. Add chicken; cook 4 to 5 minutes per side or until chicken is cooked through (165°F) and no longer pink in center. Pour any juices from skillet over chicken.

Bacon and Cheese Stuffed Chicken

MAKES 4 SERVINGS

- **4 boneless skinless chicken breasts (about 6 ounces each)**
- **½ cup (2 ounces) shredded Swiss cheese**
- **2 tablespoons real bacon bits or chopped crisp-cooked bacon**
- **2 teaspoons paprika, divided**
- **1½ teaspoons salt, divided**
- **¼ teaspoon red pepper flakes, divided**
- **2 teaspoons vegetable oil**
- **1¼ cups chicken broth**
- **⅔ cup uncooked quick-cooking brown rice**
- **½ cup sliced green onions**

1 Cut a slit in thickest part of each chicken breast forming a pocket. Place chicken between sheets of waxed paper or plastic wrap; pound to even ½-inch thickness. Combine cheese and bacon bits in small bowl; stuff into pockets, pressing edges of chicken closed over filling. Sprinkle 1 teaspoon paprika, 1 teaspoon salt and ⅛ teaspoon red pepper flakes over chicken.

2 Heat oil in large nonstick skillet over medium heat. Add chicken; cook 5 minutes per side or until chicken is cooked through (165°F) and no longer pink in center.

3 Meanwhile, combine broth, rice, remaining 1 teaspoon paprika, ½ teaspoon salt and ⅛ teaspoon red pepper flakes in medium saucepan. Bring to a boil over high heat. Reduce heat; cover and simmer 10 minutes or until liquid is absorbed. Stir green onions into rice; transfer to four serving plates and top with chicken.

Beef and Bean Stuffed Peppers

MAKES 4 SERVINGS

- 12 ounces ground beef
- 1 package (about 1 ounce) taco seasoning mix
- 1 can (about 14 ounces) diced tomatoes
- ½ (15-ounce) can black beans, rinsed and drained
- ½ cup finely chopped green onions
- 2 green bell peppers, halved vertically and stems and seeds removed
- Sour cream and chopped fresh cilantro

1. Brown beef in large saucepan over medium-high heat 6 to 8 minutes, stirring to break up meat. Drain fat. Add seasoning mix, tomatoes, beans and green onions; stir until well blended. Top with bell pepper halves, cut side down. Reduce heat to low; simmer 20 minutes or until bell peppers are just tender when pierced with a fork.
2. Place one bell pepper half on each of four plates; spoon beef mixture into peppers. Top with sour cream and cilantro.

Sticky Balsamic Chicken

MAKES 4 SERVINGS

- 2 tablespoons olive oil, divided
- ½ cup chopped shallots
- 1 cup cola beverage
- ⅓ cup balsamic vinegar
- 1½ pounds boneless skinless chicken cutlets
- 2 cloves garlic, minced
- 2 tablespoons chopped fresh basil
- ½ teaspoon salt
- ½ teaspoon black pepper

1 Spray grill grate with nonstick cooking spray. Preheat grill to medium-high heat.

2 Heat 1 tablespoon oil in large nonstick skillet over medium heat. Add shallots; cook and stir 3 minutes or until tender. Reduce heat to low. Add cola and vinegar; simmer 10 minutes or until reduced to ⅔ cup. Reserve ⅓ cup sauce in small bowl for serving; set aside.

3 Place chicken on cutting board. Rub with garlic, basil, salt and pepper; drizzle with remaining oil.

4 Grill chicken 2 to 3 minutes per side or until chicken is cooked through (165°F) and no longer pink in center, basting with remaining ⅓ cup balsamic mixture in saucepan. Serve chicken with reserved balsamic mixture.

Chicken Parmesan

MAKES 4 SERVINGS

- 2 cups marinara or tomato sauce
- 1 egg
- ¾ cup plain dry bread crumbs
- ½ cup grated Parmesan cheese
- ¼ teaspoon salt
- ¼ teaspoon black pepper
- 1½ pounds chicken tenders
- 3 tablespoons olive oil
- 8 ounces fresh mozzarella cheese, cut into thin slices

1. Preheat broiler. Spread marinara sauce in 13×9-inch baking pan.
2. Beat egg in shallow bowl. Combine bread crumbs, Parmesan, salt and pepper in another shallow bowl.
3. Dip chicken tenders into egg, letting excess drip back into bowl. Roll in crumb mixture, coating all sides.
4. Heat oil in large nonstick skillet over medium-high heat. Cook chicken in batches about 5 minutes or until golden brown, turning once.
5. Arrange chicken in single layer in baking pan. Top with mozzarella slices. Broil 6 inches from heat 5 to 7 minutes or until chicken is cooked through (165°F) and no longer pink in center and cheese is beginning to brown.

Jamaican Shrimp and Pineapple Kabobs

MAKES 4 SERVINGS

- ½ cup prepared jerk sauce
- ¼ cup pineapple preserves
- 2 tablespoons minced fresh chives
- 1 pound large raw shrimp, peeled and deveined
- ½ medium pineapple, peeled, cored and cut into 1-inch cubes
- 2 large red, green or yellow bell peppers (or a combination), cut into 1-inch pieces
- Hot cooked rice (optional)

1 Prepare grill for direct cooking. Combine jerk sauce, preserves and chives in small bowl; mix well. Reserve ½ cup sauce.

2 Thread shrimp, pineapple and bell peppers onto four skewers; brush with remaining ¼ cup sauce mixture.

3 Grill kabobs over medium-high heat 6 to 10 minutes or until shrimp turns pink and opaque, turning once. Serve with reserved sauce mixture and rice, if desired.

Garlic Beef

MAKES 4 SERVINGS

- 1 teaspoon toasted sesame oil
- 1 pound beef eye of round, trimmed, cut into thin strips
- 1 package (10 ounces) frozen chopped broccoli
- 1 tablespoon minced garlic
- 1 tablespoon soy sauce
- ¼ teaspoon black pepper

Heat oil in large nonstick skillet over high heat. Add beef, broccoli, garlic, soy sauce and pepper. Cook 15 minutes or until beef is barely pink in center, stirring occasionally.

Crisp Lemony Baked Fish

MAKES 4 SERVINGS

- 1¼ cups crushed cornflakes
- ¼ cup grated Parmesan cheese
- 2 tablespoons minced green onion
- ⅛ teaspoon black pepper
- 1 lemon
- 1 egg
- 4 small haddock fillets (about 3 ounces each)

1 Preheat oven to 400°F. Line baking sheet with parchment paper.

2 Combine cornflakes, cheese, green onion and pepper in shallow bowl. Grate lemon; stir peel into cornflake mixture. Reserve lemon.

3 Whisk egg in another shallow bowl. Dip fish into egg, letting excess drip back into bowl. Roll in cornflake mixture, coating all sides. Place fish on prepared baking sheet.

4 Bake 10 minutes or until fish begins to flake when tested with fork. Cut reserved lemon into wedges; serve with fish.

Pork Chops with Bell Peppers and Sweet Potatoes

MAKES 4 SERVINGS

- 4 pork loin chops (about 1 pound), trimmed and cut about ½ inch thick
- 1 teaspoon salt
- 1 teaspoon lemon pepper
- 1 tablespoon vegetable oil
- ½ cup beef broth or water
- 1 tablespoon lemon juice
- 1 teaspoon dried fines herbes, crushed
- 1¼ cups red or yellow bell pepper strips or a combination
- 1 cup sliced sweet potato, cut into 1-inch pieces
- ¾ cup sliced onion
- Hot cooked rice (optional)

1. Rub both sides of chops with salt and lemon pepper. Heat oil in large skillet over medium-high heat. Add pork chops; cook 5 minutes or until browned on both sides, turning once.
2. Combine broth, lemon juice and fines herbes in small bowl; pour over pork. Reduce heat to medium-low; cover and simmer 5 minutes.
3. Add bell peppers, sweet potato and onion to skillet; return to a boil. Reduce heat; cover and simmer 10 to 15 minutes or until chops are slightly pink in center (145°F) and vegetables are crisp-tender. Remove pork chops and vegetables from skillet; keep warm.
4. Bring remaining juices in skillet to a boil over high heat. Reduce heat to medium; cook and stir 6 to 8 minutes or until mixture thickens slightly. Serve pork and vegetables over rice, if desired.

Pasta & Noodles

Spicy Chicken Rigatoni

MAKES 4 SERVINGS

- 1 package (16 ounces) uncooked mezzo rigatoni or penne pasta
- ¾ cup frozen peas
- 2 tablespoons olive oil
- 2 cloves garlic, minced
- ½ teaspoon red pepper flakes
- ½ teaspoon black pepper
- 8 ounces boneless skinless chicken breasts, cut into thin strips
- 1 cup marinara sauce
- ¾ cup Alfredo sauce
- Grated Parmesan cheese (optional)

1. Cook pasta in large saucepan of salted boiling water according to package directions for al dente, adding peas during last minute of cooking. Drain and return to saucepan; keep warm.
2. Meanwhile, heat oil in large saucepan over medium-high heat. Add garlic, red pepper flakes and black pepper; cook and stir 1 minute. Add chicken; cook and stir 4 minutes or until browned.
3. Add marinara sauce and Alfredo sauce; stir until blended. Reduce heat to medium-low; cook 10 minutes, stirring occasionally or until chicken is cooked through (165°F) and no longer pink in center. Add pasta and peas; stir gently to coat. Cook 2 minutes or until heated through. Sprinkle with cheese, if desired.

Penne with Sausage and Feta

MAKES 4 SERVINGS

- 8 ounces uncooked penne or rigatoni pasta
- 3 tablespoons olive oil, divided
- 12 ounces mild Italian bulk sausage or regular sausage removed from casings
- ¼ teaspoon red pepper flakes
- 2 cups packed baby spinach
- ½ cup roasted red peppers, cut into thin strips
- 24 pitted kalamata olives, coarsely chopped
- ¼ cup chopped fresh basil
- ¼ teaspoon salt
- 1 cup (4 ounces) crumbled feta cheese with tomatoes and basil

1. Cook pasta in large saucepan of salted boiling water according to package directions for al dente. Drain and return to saucepan; keep warm.
2. Meanwhile, heat 1 tablespoon oil in large skillet over medium-high heat. Add sausage and pepper flakes; cook until sausage is cooked through, stirring to break up meat. Drain fat.
3. Add pasta, spinach, roasted peppers, olives, basil, remaining 2 tablespoons oil and salt to skillet; cook and stir until spinach has wilted slightly. Stir in cheese.

Chicken and Pasta with Creamy Caper-Herb Sauce

MAKES 4 SERVINGS

- 8 ounces uncooked egg noodles
- 1 tablespoon olive oil
- 1 pound chicken tenders
- ½ teaspoon salt
- ¼ teaspoon dried oregano
- ⅓ cup white wine
- ⅓ cup chicken broth
- 4 ounces cream cheese, cubed
- 3 tablespoons milk
- 3 tablespoons capers, drained and rinsed
- 1 teaspoon Italian seasoning
- 1 clove garlic, minced
- Grated Parmesan cheese

1. Cook noodles in large saucepan of salted boiling water according to package directions for al dente. Drain and return to saucepan; keep warm.
2. Meanwhile, heat oil in large nonstick skillet over medium heat. Add chicken; sprinkle evenly with salt and oregano. Cook 5 minutes per side or until cooked through (165°F) and no longer pink in center. Transfer chicken to plate.
3. Add wine and broth to skillet; cook and stir 30 seconds. Remove from heat. Add cream cheese, milk, capers, Italian seasoning and garlic; stir until well blended. Add chicken to skillet; cook until heated through.
4. Serve sauce and chicken over noodles. Sprinkle with Parmesan cheese.

Noodle Stir-Fry

MAKES 2 SERVINGS

- 1 package (3 ounces) ramen noodles*
- 1 tablespoon vegetable oil
- 1½ cups small broccoli florets
- ½ cup chopped red bell pepper
- ½ cup shredded carrot
- 1 green onion, chopped
- 2 tablespoons soy sauce
- 1 teaspoon packed brown sugar
- 1 teaspoon toasted sesame oil
- 1 egg, beaten

**Use any flavor; discard seasoning packet.*

1. Bring medium saucepan of water to a boil. Add noodles; cook 3 minutes, stirring frequently to separate noodles. Drain and rinse under cold water until cool. Coarsely chop noodles or cut into 3-inch lengths with kitchen scissors.
2. Heat vegetable oil in large skillet over medium heat. Add broccoli, bell pepper, carrot and green onion; stir-fry 3 minutes or until crisp-tender.
3. Add noodles, soy sauce, brown sugar and sesame oil. Push mixture to one side of skillet; add egg to other side. Cook until egg is set, stirring constantly and breaking into pieces with wooden spoon. Stir into noodle mixture.

Mediterranean Beef Skillet

MAKES 4 SERVINGS

- 8 ounces uncooked rotini pasta
- 1 pound ground beef
- ½ teaspoon salt
- ½ teaspoon dried basil
- ½ teaspoon black pepper
- 1 can (about 14 ounces) diced tomatoes with garlic and onion
- 1 can (8 ounces) tomato sauce
- 1 package (6 ounces) baby spinach, coarsely chopped
- 1 can (about 2 ounces) sliced black olives, drained
- ½ cup (2 ounces) crumbled herb-flavored feta cheese

1 Cook pasta in large saucepan of salted boiling water according to package directions for al dente. Drain and return to saucepan; keep warm.

2 Meanwhile, brown beef in large skillet over medium-high heat 6 to 8 minutes, stirring to break up meat. Drain fat. Stir in salt, basil and pepper.

3 Reduce heat to medium. Add tomatoes, tomato sauce, spinach and olives; mix well. Cook 10 minutes. Stir in pasta; cook 5 minutes or until heated through. Sprinkle with cheese.

Meaty Sausage Spaghetti

MAKES 6 TO 8 SERVINGS

- 1 tablespoon olive oil
- 1 cup chopped onion
- 2 cloves garlic, minced
- 1 package (20 ounces) bulk Italian sausage
- 1 cup chopped yellow, red and/or green bell peppers
- 1 can (about 14 ounces) crushed tomatoes
- 1 can (about 14 ounces) diced tomatoes
- 2½ teaspoons salt
- 2 teaspoons dried basil
- 1 teaspoon dried oregano
- ¼ teaspoon black pepper
- 1 package (16 ounces) uncooked spaghetti, broken in half
- 2½ to 3 cups water, divided
- Grated Parmesan cheese

1. Heat oil in large saucepan or Dutch oven over medium-high heat. Add onion and garlic; cook and stir 3 minutes or until softened. Add sausage; cook about 8 minutes or until browned, stirring to break up meat. Drain fat. Add bell peppers; cook and stir 2 minutes. Add crushed tomatoes, diced tomatoes, salt, basil, oregano and pepper; mix well.
2. Add pasta and 2½ cups water to saucepan; stir pasta gently to allow some liquid to get between strands. Bring to a boil. Reduce heat to medium; cover and cook 15 minutes, stirring occasionally to separate pasta.
3. Uncover; add additional water if pasta seems dry. Test pasta for doneness; continue to cook 2 to 3 minutes or until pasta reaches desired doneness, stirring frequently. Adjust seasonings. Sprinkle with cheese.

Note

You can also use 1 pound of ground beef, pork, meatloaf mix or even plant-based meat substitute in place of the sausage.

Greek Chicken and Pasta

MAKES 4 SERVINGS

- 8 ounces uncooked fettuccine or whole wheat fettuccine
- 1 jar (6 ounces) marinated artichoke hearts
- 1 tablespoon olive oil
- 1 red bell pepper, cut into very thin strips
- 3 cloves garlic, minced
- 1 pound boneless skinless chicken breasts, cut into bite-size pieces
- 1 tablespoon plus 1 teaspoon lemon juice
- 2 teaspoons dried oregano
- 1 teaspoon grated lemon peel
- ½ teaspoon salt
- ¼ teaspoon dried mint (optional)
- ¼ teaspoon black pepper
- ⅓ cup sliced pitted black olives
- ¼ cup crumbled feta cheese

1. Cook pasta in large saucepan of salted boiling water according to package directions for al dente. Drain and place in large bowl; keep warm.
2. Meanwhile, drain artichoke hearts, reserving marinade. Cut artichoke hearts into quarters; set aside.
3. Heat oil in large skillet over medium heat. Add bell pepper and garlic; cook and stir over medium heat until tender. Transfer vegetables to medium bowl.
4. Add chicken to skillet; cook and stir 2 to 3 minutes or until chicken is almost cooked through.
5. Return vegetable mixture to skillet. Add reserved artichoke marinade, lemon juice, oregano, lemon peel, salt, mint, if desired, and black pepper; bring to a boil. Reduce heat; simmer, uncovered, 1 to 2 minutes or until chicken is cooked through (165°F) and no longer pink in center. Stir in artichoke hearts and olives. Add mixture to pasta; toss to coat. Sprinkle with cheese.

Smoked Sausage Mac and Cheese

MAKES 4 TO 6 SERVINGS

- 1 tablespoon olive oil
- 1 medium onion, finely chopped
- 1 package (about 12 ounces) smoked turkey sausage, cut into ¼-inch slices
- 1 package (16 ounces) uncooked cavatappi pasta
- 4 cups water
- 2 teaspoons salt, divided
- 4 tablespoons butter, divided
- 1 clove garlic, minced
- 1 cup panko bread crumbs
- 4 cups (16 ounces) shredded Cheddar cheese
- 1 cup (4 ounces) shredded Monterey Jack cheese
- 1 can (12 ounces) evaporated milk
- Black pepper

1 Heat oil in large saucepan or Dutch oven over medium-high heat. Add onion; cook 5 to 7 minutes or until golden brown. Add sausage; cook and stir 5 minutes or until lightly browned. Add pasta, water and 1½ teaspoons salt; cover and cook 13 to 15 minutes or until pasta is al dente, stirring occasionally.

2 Meanwhile, melt 2 tablespoons butter in medium skillet over medium-high heat. Add garlic; cook and stir 30 seconds. Add panko and remaining ½ teaspoon salt; cook and stir 2 minutes or until panko is golden brown. Remove from heat.

3 Uncover pasta and reduce heat to medium-low. Stir in cheeses, evaporated milk and remaining 2 tablespoons butter; cook and stir 1 to 2 minutes or until cheese is melted and pasta is creamy. Season with black pepper; sprinkle with panko.

Puttanesca Pasta

MAKES 4 TO 6 SERVINGS

- 2 tablespoons olive oil
- 2 to 3 anchovy fillets, chopped
- 2 tablespoons tomato paste
- 3 cloves garlic, minced
- 2 cans (about 14 ounces each) diced tomatoes
- 1 can (14 ounces) tomato sauce
- 1 teaspoon salt
- 1 teaspoon dried oregano
- 1 teaspoon dried basil
- ¼ teaspoon black pepper
- ½ cup pitted Greek olives, coarsely chopped
- 2 tablespoons rinsed and drained capers
- ½ to 1½ teaspoons red pepper flakes
- 1 package (16 ounces) uncooked angel hair or vermicelli pasta

1 Heat oil in large skillet over medium-low heat. Add anchovies, tomato paste and garlic; cook and stir 3 minutes or until fragrant. Stir in tomatoes, tomato sauce, salt, oregano, basil and pepper. Increase heat to medium; cook 20 minutes or until sauce is thickened, stirring frequently. Stir in olives, capers and red pepper flakes; cook 5 minutes.

2 Meanwhile, cook pasta in large saucepan of salted boiling water according to package directions for al dente. Drain; toss with sauce.

Bowtie Pasta with Chicken and Bacon

MAKES 4 SERVINGS

- 3 cups uncooked bowtie pasta (farfalle)
- 4 slices bacon, chopped
- 1 pound boneless skinless chicken breasts, cut into 1-inch pieces
- 1 can (about 14 ounces) Italian-style diced tomatoes
- ½ teaspoon salt
- ¼ teaspoon black pepper
- ½ cup chicken broth or water
- 4 ounces cream cheese, cubed
- 4 tablespoons grated Parmesan cheese, divided

1. Cook pasta in large saucepan of salted boiling water according to package directions for al dente. Drain and return to saucepan; keep warm.
2. Meanwhile, cook bacon in large skillet over medium-high heat until almost crisp. Remove to paper towel-lined plate. Drain all but 1 tablespoon drippings from skillet.
3. Add chicken to skillet; cook over medium heat about 6 minutes or until cooked through (165°F) and no longer pink in center, stirring occasionally. Add tomatoes, salt and pepper; cook and stir 1 minute. Add broth, cream cheese and 2 tablespoons Parmesan cheese; cook and stir about 3 minutes or until cream cheese is melted.
4. Add chicken mixture to pasta; toss gently to coat. Sprinkle with remaining 2 tablespoons Parmesan cheese.

Easy Taco Pasta Skillet

MAKES 6 SERVINGS

- 1 pound ground beef
- 1 onion, chopped
- 1 package (about 1 ounce) taco seasoning mix
- 2 cups water
- 1 jar (16 ounces) medium salsa
- 1 can (4 ounces) diced mild green chiles
- ¼ teaspoon salt
- 8 ounces uncooked rotini pasta
- Shredded Cheddar or Mexican blend cheese (optional)

1. Cook beef and onion in large skillet over medium-high heat 6 to 8 minutes or until beef is browned, stirring to break up meat. Drain fat. Add taco seasoning mix; cook and stir 1 minute.
2. Stir in water, salsa, chiles and salt; mix well. Stir in pasta; bring to a simmer. Reduce heat to low; cover and cook about 12 minutes or until pasta is tender. Sprinkle with cheese, if desired.

Bowtie Zucchini

MAKES 4 TO 6 SERVINGS

- 1 package (12 to 16 ounces) bowtie pasta (farfalle)
- ¼ cup (½ stick) butter or olive oil
- 1 cup chopped onion
- 2 cloves garlic, minced
- 5 small zucchini, cut into thin strips
- 1 teaspoon salt
- ⅔ cup whipping cream
- 3 tablespoons grated Parmesan cheese
- Black pepper

1 Preheat oven to 350°F. Cook pasta in large saucepan of salted boiling water according to package directions for al dente. Drain and return to saucepan; keep warm.

2 Meanwhile, melt butter in large skillet over medium-high heat. Add onion and garlic; cook and stir 3 minutes or until onion is translucent. Add zucchini and salt; cook and stir 8 to 10 minutes until tender.

3 Add cream; cook and stir until slightly thickened. Pour mixture over pasta; stir to coat. Stir in cheese and season with pepper. Transfer mixture to 2-quart baking dish. Cover and bake 15 minutes or until heated through.

Udon Noodles with Chicken and Spinach

MAKES 4 SERVINGS

- 1 package (8 ounces) uncooked udon noodles
- 3 tablespoons vegetable oil, divided
- 4 boneless skinless chicken thighs (about 12 ounces), cut into bite-size pieces
- 1 tablespoon grated fresh ginger
- 2 cloves garlic, minced
- 1 cup chicken broth
- 1 package (6 ounces) baby spinach, coarsely chopped
- 2 green onions, chopped
- 1 tablespoon soy sauce

1. Cook noodles according to package directions. Drain and return to saucepan.
2. Meanwhile, heat 2 tablespoons oil in large nonstick skillet over medium heat. Add chicken; cook and stir 5 to 6 minutes or until cooked through (165°F). Transfer to paper towel-lined plate.
3. Add remaining 1 tablespoon oil to skillet. Add ginger and garlic; cook over low heat 20 seconds or until garlic begins to turn light brown. Add broth; bring to a simmer.
4. Stir in spinach and green onions; cook and stir 2 to 3 minutes or until spinach wilts. Stir chicken and noodles into spinach mixture. Stir in soy sauce. Serve immediately.

Creamy Macaroni and Broccoli

MAKES 4 SERVINGS

- 12 ounces uncooked elbow macaroni
- 2 cups small broccoli florets
- 6 tablespoons butter
- 6 tablespoons all-purpose flour
- 1 teaspoon salt
- 2 cups milk
- ¼ cup plus 2 tablespoons grated Romano cheese
- Dash ground nutmeg
- Shaved Romano cheese (optional)

1. Cook macaroni in large saucepan of salted boiling water according to package directions for al dente, adding broccoli during last 4 minutes of cooking. Drain and return to saucepan; keep warm.
2. Melt butter in medium saucepan over medium heat. Whisk in flour and salt; cook and stir 2 minutes. Gradually add milk, whisking constantly until well blended and smooth. Cook and stir 3 to 4 minutes or until slightly thickened. Remove from heat. Stir in grated cheese and nutmeg.
3. Add macaroni and broccoli to sauce; mix well. Sprinkle with shaved Romano cheese, if desired.

Tortellini with Artichokes, Olives and Feta

MAKES 4 TO 6 SERVINGS

- 2 packages (9 ounces each) refrigerated cheese-filled spinach tortellini
- 2 jars (4 ounces each) marinated artichoke heart quarters, drained*
- ½ cup sliced pitted black olives
- 2 medium carrots, diagonally sliced
- ½ cup crumbled feta cheese
- ½ cup cheese-garlic Italian salad dressing
- Black pepper

**For additional flavor, add some artichoke marinade to tortellini with salad dressing.*

1. Cook tortellini according to package directions.
2. Meanwhile, combine artichoke hearts, olives, carrots and feta in large bowl. Add salad dressing; toss lightly. Stir in tortellini; season to taste with pepper.

Lemon Broccoli Pasta

MAKES 4 TO 6 SERVINGS

- 2 tablespoons butter
- ½ cup sliced green onions
- 2 cloves garlic, minced
- 4 cups vegetable broth
- 2 teaspoons grated lemon peel
- ½ teaspoon salt
- ⅛ teaspoon black pepper
- 8 ounces uncooked angel hair pasta
- 2 cups fresh or frozen broccoli florets
- ⅔ cup sour cream
- ¼ cup grated Parmesan cheese

1. Melt butter in large saucepan over medium heat. Add green onions and garlic; cook and stir 3 minutes or until onions are tender.
2. Add broth, lemon peel, salt and pepper to saucepan; bring to a boil over high heat. Stir in pasta and broccoli; return to a boil. Reduce heat to low; cook about 6 minutes or until pasta is al dente, stirring frequently.
3. Remove from heat; stir in sour cream until well blended. Let stand 5 minutes; top with cheese.

Rice, Grains & Beans

Quinoa Chili

MAKES 4 SERVINGS

- 2 tablespoons vegetable oil
- 1 onion, chopped
- 1 red bell pepper, chopped
- 1 large carrot, sliced
- 1 stalk celery, diced
- 1 jalapeño pepper, finely chopped
- 1 tablespoon minced garlic
- 1 tablespoon chili powder
- 2 teaspoons ground cumin
- 1 teaspoon salt
- 1 can (28 ounces) crushed tomatoes
- 1 can (about 15 ounces) kidney beans, rinsed and drained
- 1 cup water
- 1 cup fresh or thawed frozen corn
- 1 cup cooked quinoa*
- Optional toppings: diced avocado, shredded Cheddar cheese and sliced green onions

***Cook ½ cup uncooked quinoa according to package directions.**

1 Heat oil in large saucepan over medium-high heat. Add onion, bell pepper, carrot and celery; cook 5 minutes or until vegetables are softened, stirring occasionally. Add jalapeño, garlic, chili powder, cumin and salt; cook 1 minute or until fragrant.

2 Stir in tomatoes, beans, water, corn and quinoa; bring to a boil. Reduce heat to medium; cover and simmer 20 minutes, stirring occasionally. Serve with desired toppings.

Minestrone Soup

MAKES 4 TO 6 SERVINGS

- 1 tablespoon olive oil
- ½ cup chopped onion
- 1 stalk celery, diced
- 1 carrot, diced
- 2 cloves garlic, minced
- 4 cups vegetable broth or water
- 1 bay leaf
- ¾ teaspoon salt
- ½ teaspoon dried basil
- ½ teaspoon dried oregano
- ¼ teaspoon dried thyme
- ¼ teaspoon sugar
- Ground black pepper
- 1 can (about 15 ounces) dark red kidney beans, rinsed and drained
- 1 can (about 15 ounces) navy beans or cannellini beans, rinsed and drained
- 1 can (about 14 ounces) diced tomatoes
- 1 cup diced zucchini (about 1 small)
- ½ cup uncooked small shell pasta
- ½ cup fresh or frozen cut green beans
- ¼ cup dry red wine
- 1 cup packed chopped fresh spinach
- Grated Parmesan cheese (optional)

1. Heat oil in large saucepan or Dutch oven over medium-high heat. Add onion, celery, carrot and garlic; cook and stir 5 to 7 minutes or until vegetables are tender. Add broth, bay leaf, salt, basil, oregano, thyme, sugar and pepper; bring to a boil.
2. Stir in kidney beans, navy beans, tomatoes, zucchini, pasta, green beans and wine; cook 10 minutes, stirring occasionally.
3. Add spinach; cook 2 minutes or until pasta and zucchini are tender. Remove and discard bay leaf. Serve with cheese, if desired.

Quinoa Burrito Bowls

MAKES 4 SERVINGS

- 1 cup uncooked quinoa
- 2 cups water
- 2 tablespoons lime juice, divided
- 2 teaspoons vegetable oil
- 1 small onion, diced
- 1 red bell pepper, diced
- 1 clove garlic, minced
- ½ cup canned black beans, rinsed and drained
- ½ cup thawed frozen corn
- ¼ cup sour cream
- Shredded lettuce
- Lime wedges (optional)

1. Place quinoa in fine-mesh strainer; rinse well under cold water. Bring 2 cups water to a boil in small saucepan; stir in quinoa. Reduce heat to low; cover and simmer 10 to 15 minutes or until quinoa is tender and water is absorbed. Stir in 1 tablespoon lime juice. Cover and keep warm.
2. Meanwhile, heat oil in large skillet over medium heat. Add onion and bell pepper; cook and stir 5 minutes or until softened. Add garlic; cook 1 minute. Add black beans and corn; cook 3 to 5 minutes or until heated through.
3. Combine sour cream and remaining 1 tablespoon lime juice in small bowl; mix well.
4. Divide quinoa among four serving bowls; top with black bean mixture, lettuce and sour cream mixture. Garnish with lime wedges.

Cannellini Chicken Skillet

MAKES 4 SERVINGS

- 2 tablespoons olive oil
- 2 boneless skinless chicken breasts (about 6 ounces each), cut into 1-inch chunks
- 1 can (about 14 ounces) diced tomatoes
- 1 cup frozen chopped spinach
- 2 cloves garlic, chopped
- 1 tablespoon chopped fresh rosemary *or* 1 teaspoon dried rosemary
- 1 teaspoon salt
- ½ teaspoon red pepper flakes
- 1 can (about 15 ounces) cannellini beans, rinsed and drained
- 1 cup grape tomatoes, cut in half

1 Heat oil in large skillet over medium-high heat. Add chicken; cook and stir 8 minutes or until chicken is cooked through (165°F) and no longer pink in center.

2 Add diced tomatoes, spinach, garlic, rosemary, salt and red pepper flakes to skillet; cook and stir 10 minutes or until spinach is thawed. Add beans and grape tomatoes; cook 2 minutes or until beans are heated through.

Chicken Fried Rice

MAKES 4 SERVINGS

- 2 tablespoons vegetable oil, divided
- 12 ounces boneless skinless chicken breasts, cut into ½-inch cubes
- Salt and black pepper
- 2 tablespoons butter
- 2 cloves garlic, minced
- ½ sweet onion, diced
- 1 medium carrot, diced
- 2 green onions, thinly sliced, plus additional for garnish
- 3 eggs
- 4 cups cooked rice*
- 3 tablespoons soy sauce
- 2 tablespoons sesame seeds

**For rice, cook 1½ cups rice according to package directions without oil or butter. Spread hot rice on large rimmed baking sheet; cool to room temperature. Refrigerate several hours or overnight.*

1 Heat 1 tablespoon oil in large skillet over medium-high heat. Add chicken; season with salt and pepper. Cook and stir 5 to 6 minutes or until cooked through (165°F) and no longer pink in center. Add butter and garlic; cook and stir 1 minute or until butter is melted. Transfer to medium bowl.

2 Add sweet onion, carrot and two green onions to skillet; cook and stir over high heat 3 minutes or until vegetables are softened. Add to bowl with chicken.

3 Heat remaining 1 tablespoon oil in same skillet. Crack eggs into skillet; cook and stir 45 seconds or until eggs are scrambled but still moist. Return chicken and vegetable mixture to skillet with rice, soy sauce and sesame seeds; cook and stir 2 minutes or until well blended and heated through. Season with additional salt and pepper; garnish with additional green onion.

Greek Salad Bowl

MAKES 4 SERVINGS

- 1 cup uncooked pearled farro
- 2½ cups water
- 1¼ teaspoons dried oregano or Greek seasoning, divided
- ½ teaspoon salt, divided
- ¼ cup extra virgin olive oil
- 2 tablespoons red wine vinegar
- 1 clove garlic, minced
- ⅛ teaspoon black pepper
- 2 cucumbers, julienned, cubed or thinly sliced*
- ½ red onion, thinly sliced*
- 2 medium tomatoes, diced
- 1 can (about 15 ounces) chickpeas, rinsed and drained
- 4 ounces feta cheese, cubed or crumbled

**This is a great recipe to use a spiralizer if you have one. Cut the ends off the cucumbers and spiral slice with the thin ribbon blade. Spiral the red onion with the thin ribbon blade and chop into desired pieces.*

1. Rinse farro under cold water; place in medium saucepan. Add 2½ cups water, 1 teaspoon oregano and ¼ teaspoon salt. Bring to a boil over high heat. Reduce heat to medium-low; simmer, uncovered, 20 minutes or until farro is tender. Drain any additional water.
2. Meanwhile, whisk oil, vinegar, garlic, remaining ¼ teaspoon salt, remaining ¼ teaspoon oregano and pepper in small bowl.
3. Divide farro among four bowls; arrange cucumber, onion, tomatoes, chickpeas and feta around farro. Drizzle with dressing.

Southwestern Chicken and Black Bean Skillet

MAKES 4 SERVINGS

- 1 teaspoon ground cumin
- 1 teaspoon chili powder
- ½ teaspoon salt
- 4 boneless skinless chicken breasts (about 6 ounces each)
- 2 teaspoons vegetable oil
- 1 cup chopped onion
- 1 red bell pepper, chopped
- 1 can (about 15 ounces) black beans, rinsed and drained
- ½ cup chunky salsa
- Lime wedges
- ¼ cup chopped fresh cilantro or green onions (optional)

1 Combine cumin, chili powder and salt in small bowl; sprinkle evenly over both sides of chicken.

2 Heat oil in large skillet over medium-high heat. Add chicken; cook 4 minutes, turning once. Transfer chicken to plate.

3 Add onion to same skillet; cook and stir 1 minute. Add bell pepper; cook 5 minutes, stirring occasionally. Stir in beans and salsa.

4 Place chicken on top of bean mixture; cover and cook 6 to 7 minutes or until chicken is cooked through (165°F) and no longer pink in center. Serve with lime wedges and garnish with cilantro.

Hoppin' Shrimp and Brown Rice

MAKES 4 SERVINGS

- 1 bag boil-in-bag instant brown rice
- 2 cups frozen black-eyed peas *or* 1 can (15 ounces) black-eyed peas, rinsed and drained
- 2 cups vegetable broth
- 2 cups salsa with jalapeños
- 1 can (about 14 ounces) diced tomatoes
- 1 bag (12 ounces) cooked baby shrimp
- 1 box (10 ounces) frozen whole okra
- 4 stalks celery, chopped
- ¼ cup chopped red onion
- ¼ cup chopped cilantro
- Juice of ½ lime
- ½ teaspoon black pepper
- Lime wedges (optional)

1 Prepare rice according to package directions.

2 Meanwhile, combine black-eyed peas, broth, salsa, tomatoes, shrimp, okra, celery, onion, cilantro, lime juice and black pepper in large skillet; bring to a simmer over medium-high heat. Simmer 20 minutes or until heated through, stirring occasionally.

3 Place 1½ cups shrimp mixture in serving bowl; top with ½ cup rice. Garnish with lime wedges.

Brown Rice with Chickpeas, Spinach and Feta

MAKES 4 SERVINGS

- 1 tablespoon olive oil
- ½ cup diced celery
- 2 cups water
- 1 can (about 15 ounces) chickpeas, rinsed and drained
- 1 package (10 ounces) frozen chopped spinach, thawed and squeezed dry
- ½ cup uncooked instant brown rice
- 1 teaspoon Greek or Italian seasoning
- 1 clove garlic, minced
- ½ teaspoon salt
- ⅛ teaspoon black pepper
- ½ cup crumbled feta cheese
- 1 tablespoon lemon juice

1 Heat oil in large skillet over medium-high heat. Add celery; cook 6 to 7 minutes or until softened and browned in spots, stirring occasionally.

2 Add water, chickpeas, spinach, rice, Greek seasoning, garlic, salt and pepper; cover and bring to a boil. Reduce heat to low; cover and simmer 12 minutes or until rice is tender. Remove from heat. Add feta and lemon juice; mix gently.

Sandwiches, Tacos & Pizza

BLT Supreme

MAKES 2 SERVINGS

- **6 to 8 slices thick-cut bacon**
- **⅓ cup mayonnaise**
- **1½ teaspoons minced chipotle pepper in adobo sauce**
- **1 teaspoon lime juice**
- **1 ripe avocado**
- **⅛ teaspoon salt**
- **⅛ teaspoon black pepper**
- **4 leaves romaine lettuce**
- **½ baguette, cut into 2 (8-inch) lengths *or* 2 hoagie rolls, split and toasted**
- **6 to 8 slices tomato**

1 Cook bacon in skillet or oven until crisp-chewy. Drain on paper towel-lined plate.

2 Meanwhile, combine mayonnaise, chipotle pepper and lime juice in small bowl; mix well. Coarsely mash avocado in another small bowl; stir in salt and black pepper. Cut lettuce crosswise into ¼-inch strips.

3 For each sandwich, spread heaping tablespoon mayonnaise mixture on bottom half of baguette; top with one fourth of lettuce. Arrange 3 to 4 slices bacon over lettuce; spread 2 tablespoons mashed avocado over bacon. Drizzle with heaping tablespoon mayonnaise mixture. Top with 3 to 4 tomato slices, one fourth of lettuce and 3 to 4 slices bacon. Close sandwich with top half of baguette.

Classic Turkey Tacos

MAKES 12 TACOS

- 2 teaspoons vegetable oil
- 1 pound ground turkey
- 2 tablespoons tomato paste
- 2 cloves garlic, minced
- 1 package (about 1 ounce) taco seasoning mix
- 1 cup fresh or thawed frozen corn
- 1 cup canned kidney beans, rinsed and drained
- ½ cup water
- 12 (6-inch) flour tortillas, warmed according to package directions
- 3 avocados, sliced
- 1 cup grape tomatoes, sliced
- ½ cup sliced red onion

1 Heat oil in large nonstick skillet over high heat. Add turkey; cook about 5 minutes or until turkey is no longer pink, stirring to break up meat. Add tomato paste, garlic and seasoning; cook and stir 1 minute. Stir in corn, beans and water. Reduce heat to medium; simmer 5 minutes.

2 Serve turkey mixture in tortillas with avocados, tomatoes and onions.

Spinach and Artichoke Grilled Pizza

MAKES 4 SERVINGS

- 1 tablespoon olive oil
- 2 cloves garlic, minced
- 3 cups baby spinach, coarsely chopped
- ½ cup pizza sauce
- 1 prepared whole wheat thin pizza crust (10 ounces)
- 1 cup chopped cooked chicken
- ½ cup chopped canned artichoke hearts, rinsed and drained
- 1 cup (4 ounces) shredded mozzarella cheese

1. Prepare grill for direct cooking over medium heat.
2. Meanwhile, heat oil in medium skillet over medium heat. Add garlic; cook and stir 30 seconds. Stir in spinach; cook and stir until spinach is wilted. Remove from heat; drain any excess liquid from skillet.
3. Spread pizza sauce over crust to within 1 inch of edge. Top with spinach mixture, chicken, artichokes and cheese. Place pizza crust directly on grill grate. Grill over medium heat 3 to 5 minutes or until crust is browned and cheese is melted.

Tuscan Portobello Melt

MAKES 2 SERVINGS

- 1 portobello mushroom cap, thinly sliced
- ½ small red onion, thinly sliced
- ½ cup grape tomatoes
- 1 tablespoon olive oil
- 1 teaspoon balsamic vinegar
- ⅛ teaspoon salt
- ⅛ teaspoon dried thyme
- ⅛ teaspoon black pepper
- 2 tablespoons butter, softened, divided
- 4 slices sourdough bread
- 2 slices provolone cheese
- 2 teaspoons Dijon mustard
- 2 slices Monterey Jack cheese

1. Preheat broiler. Combine mushroom, onion and tomatoes in small baking pan. Drizzle with oil and vinegar; sprinkle with salt, thyme and pepper. Toss to coat and spread vegetables in single layer in pan.
2. Broil 6 minutes or until vegetables are softened and browned, stirring once.
3. Heat medium skillet over medium heat. Spread half of butter over one side of each bread slice. Place buttered side down in skillet; cook 2 minutes or until bread is toasted. Transfer bread to cutting board, toasted sides up.
4. Place provolone cheese on two bread slices; spread mustard over cheese. Top with vegetables, Monterey Jack cheese and remaining bread slices, toasted sides down. Spread remaining half of butter over outside of sandwiches. Cook in same skillet over medium heat 5 minutes or until bread is toasted and cheese is melted, turning once.

Tuna Melt

MAKES 4 SERVINGS

- ¾ cup mayonnaise
- 2 teaspoons lemon juice
- 1 teaspoon salt
- ⅛ teaspoon black pepper
- 1 can (12 ounces) solid white albacore tuna, drained
- 1 can (12 ounces) chunk light tuna, drained
- 1 stalk celery, finely chopped (about ½ cup)
- ¼ cup minced red onion
- 8 slices bread
- 8 slices Cheddar or American cheese
- 2 tablespoons butter
- Optional toppings: tomato slices, onion slices, pickles and/or lettuce leaves

1 Combine mayonnaise, lemon juice, salt and pepper in large bowl. Add tuna, celery and red onion; mix well.

2 Divide tuna salad among bread slices; top each with cheese. Heat 1 tablespoon butter in large skillet over medium heat until melted. Add half of sandwiches; cover and cook until bread is toasted and cheese is melted. Repeat with remaining butter and sandwiches. Garnish with desired toppings.

Chicken Bacon Quesadillas

MAKES 4 SERVINGS

- 4 teaspoons vegetable oil, divided
- 4 (8-inch) flour tortillas
- 1 cup (4 ounces) shredded Colby-Jack cheese
- 2 cups coarsely chopped cooked chicken
- 4 slices bacon, crisp-cooked and coarsely chopped
- ½ cup pico de gallo, plus additional for serving
- Sour cream and guacamole (optional)

1. Heat large nonstick skillet over medium heat; brush with 1 teaspoon oil. Place one tortilla in skillet; sprinkle with ¼ cup cheese. Spread ½ cup chicken over one half of tortilla; top with one fourth of bacon and 2 tablespoons pico de gallo.
2. Cook 1 to 2 minutes or until cheese is melted and bottom of tortilla is lightly browned. Fold tortilla over filling, pressing with spatula. Transfer to cutting board. Repeat with remaining ingredients. Cut quesadillas into wedges. Serve with additional pico de gallo, sour cream and guacamole, if desired.

Smashed Burgers

MAKES 4 SERVINGS

- **4 slices bacon, cut in half**
- **1 pound ground beef**
- **Salt and black pepper**
- **4 slices sharp Cheddar cheese**
- **4 eggs (optional)**
- **4 brioche rolls or hamburger buns, split**
- **Lettuce leaves**

1 Cook bacon in large skillet over medium-high heat until crisp. Drain on paper towel-lined plate. Drain all but 1 tablespoon drippings from skillet.

2 Divide beef into four portions and shape lightly into loose balls. Place in same skillet over medium-high heat. Smash with spatula to flatten into thin patties; sprinkle with salt and pepper. Cook 2 to 3 minutes or until edges and bottoms are browned. Flip burgers; top with cheese. Cook 2 to 3 minutes for medium rare or to desired doneness. Remove to plates.

3 If desired, crack eggs into hot skillet. Cook over medium heat 3 minutes or until whites are opaque and yolks are desired degree of doneness, flipping once, if desired, for over easy. Place lettuce and burgers on rolls; top with eggs and bacon.

Turkey Sloppy Joes

MAKES 8 SERVINGS

- 1 cup ketchup
- 2 tablespoons packed brown sugar
- 2 tablespoons Worcestershire sauce
- 2 tablespoons yellow mustard
- 2 tablespoons cider vinegar
- 1 tablespoon olive oil
- 2 pounds ground turkey
- 1 medium sweet onion
- 1 red bell pepper, chopped
- 1 clove garlic, minced
- 2 teaspoons chili powder
- ½ teaspoon salt
- ½ teaspoon ground cumin
- ¼ teaspoon black pepper
- 8 hamburger buns

1 Combine ketchup, brown sugar, Worcestershire sauce, mustard and vinegar in medium bowl.

2 Heat oil in large skillet over medium-high heat. Add turkey, onion, bell pepper and garlic; cook 10 minutes or until turkey is no longer pink, stirring to break up meat. Add chili powder, salt, cumin and black pepper; cook and stir 1 minute.

3 Add ketchup mixture; mix well. Cook 10 minutes, stirring occasionally. Serve on buns.

Soft Tacos with Chicken

MAKES 8 TACOS

- 8 (6- or 7-inch) corn tortillas
- 2 tablespoons butter
- 1 medium onion, chopped
- 1½ cups shredded cooked chicken
- 1 can (4 ounces) diced mild green chiles
- 2 tablespoons chopped fresh cilantro
- 1 cup sour cream
- Salt and black pepper
- 1½ cups (6 ounces) shredded Monterey Jack cheese
- 1 avocado, sliced
- Green taco sauce

1. Stack and wrap tortillas in foil. Warm in 350°F oven 15 minutes or until heated through.
2. Meanwhile, melt butter in large skillet over medium heat. Add onion; cook and stir 5 minutes or until tender. Add chicken, chiles and cilantro; cook and stir 3 minutes or until mixture is hot. Reduce heat to low. Stir in sour cream; cook until heated through, stirring constantly (do not boil). Season to taste with salt and pepper.
3. Spoon about 3 tablespoons chicken mixture down center of each tortilla; sprinkle with 2 tablespoons cheese. Top with avocado; drizzle with taco sauce. Sprinkle tacos with remaining cheese. Roll tortillas into cone shapes or fold in half.

Taco Pizza

MAKES 4 SERVINGS

- 1 package (about 14 ounces) refrigerated pizza dough
- 1 pound ground turkey
- 1 cup chopped onion
- 1 can (8 ounces) tomato sauce
- 1 package (about 1 ounce) taco seasoning mix
- 2 plum tomatoes, thinly sliced, *or* 1 cup chopped tomato
- 1 cup (4 ounces) shredded Cheddar cheese
- 1½ cups shredded lettuce

1 Preheat oven to 425°F. Spray 12-inch pizza pan with nonstick cooking spray. Unroll pizza dough; press into prepared pan. Build up edges slightly. Prick dough with fork. Bake 7 to 10 minutes or until lightly browned.

2 Meanwhile, cook turkey and onion in large skillet 6 to 8 minutes or until turkey is no longer pink, stirring to break up meat. Add tomato sauce and taco seasoning mix; bring to a boil. Reduce heat; simmer 2 to 3 minutes. Spoon turkey mixture on pizza crust. Bake 5 minutes.

3 Arrange tomatoes over turkey mixture. Sprinkle with cheese. Bake 2 to 3 minutes or until cheese melts. Top with lettuce. Cut into wedges to serve.

Grilled Italian Chicken Panini

MAKES 6 SERVINGS

- **6 small portobello mushroom caps (about 6 ounces)**
- **½ cup plus 2 tablespoons balsamic vinaigrette**
- **1 loaf (1 pound) Italian bread, cut into 12 slices**
- **12 slices provolone cheese**
- **1½ cups chopped cooked chicken**
- **1 jar (12 ounces) roasted red peppers, drained**

1. Brush mushrooms with 2 tablespoons vinaigrette. Cook mushrooms in large nonstick skillet over medium-high heat 5 to 7 minutes or until softened, turning occasionally. Cut into ½-inch slices.
2. For each sandwich, top one bread slice with one cheese slice, ¼ cup chicken, mushrooms, roasted peppers, another cheese slice and another bread slice. Brush outsides of sandwiches with remaining vinaigrette.
3. Heat grill pan over medium heat or preheat panini maker. Cook sandwiches 4 to 6 minutes or until cheese is melted and bread is golden brown, turning once.

Tip

A rotisserie chicken will yield just enough chopped chicken for this recipe.

Jamaican Jerk Turkey Burgers with Mango Salsa

MAKES 4 SERVINGS

- 1 pound ground turkey
- ⅓ cup dry bread crumbs
- ¼ cup finely chopped red onion
- 1 egg
- 2 teaspoons Jamaican jerk seasoning
- ½ teaspoon salt
- 1 tablespoon vegetable oil
- 4 sandwich thins or hamburger buns
- 1 mango, peeled and diced
- ¼ cup pico de gallo

1. Combine turkey, bread crumbs, red onion, egg, jerk seasoning and salt in large bowl. Shape into four ½-inch-thick patties.
2. Heat oil in large skillet over medium heat. Add patties; cook 4 to 5 minutes per side or until no longer pink. Place one burger on bottom of sandwich thin.
3. Stir mango into pico de gallo in small bowl; spoon over burgers. Top with remaining sandwich thin.

Pizza Sandwich

MAKES 4 TO 6 SERVINGS

- 1 loaf (12 ounces) focaccia
- ½ cup pizza sauce
- 20 slices pepperoni
- 8 slices (1 ounce each) mozzarella cheese
- 1 can (2¼ ounces) sliced mushrooms, drained
- Red pepper flakes (optional)
- Olive oil

1. Cut focaccia horizontally in half. Spread cut sides of both halves with pizza sauce. Layer bottom half with pepperoni, cheese and mushrooms; sprinkle with red pepper flakes, if desired. Cover with top half of focaccia. Brush sandwich lightly with oil.
2. Heat large nonstick skillet over medium heat. Add sandwich; press down with spatula or weigh down with small plate. Cook sandwich 4 to 5 minutes per side or until cheese is melted and sandwich is golden brown. Cut into wedges to serve.

Easy Fish Tacos

MAKES 4 SERVINGS

- 12 frozen fish sticks (8 ounces total)
- 3 tablespoons salsa
- 2 tablespoons mayonnaise
- 4 (8-inch) flour tortillas, warmed
- 4 lettuce leaves
- ½ cup (2 ounces) shredded Cheddar cheese
- 1 cup grape tomatoes, quartered

1. Bake fish sticks according to package directions.
2. Mix salsa and mayonnaise in small bowl.
3. Line tortillas with lettuce leaves. Place three fish sticks on each tortilla; top evenly with salsa mixture, cheese and tomatoes.

Barbecue Chicken Pizza

MAKES 4 TO 6 SERVINGS

- 1 tablespoon olive oil
- 6 ounces boneless skinless chicken breasts, cut into strips (about 2×¼ inch)
- ¼ teaspoon salt
- ⅛ teaspoon black pepper
- 6 tablespoons barbecue sauce, divided
- 1 ball (16 ounces) refrigerated pizza dough, at room temperature
- ⅔ cup shredded mozzarella cheese, divided
- ½ cup shredded smoked Gouda cheese, divided
- ½ red onion, cut vertically into ⅛-inch slices
- 2 tablespoons chopped fresh cilantro

1. Preheat oven to 450°F. Line baking sheet with parchment paper.
2. Heat oil in large skillet over medium-high heat. Add chicken and sprinkle with salt and pepper; cook 5 minutes or just until cooked though, stirring occasionally. Remove chicken to medium bowl. Add 2 tablespoons barbecue sauce; stir to coat.
3. Roll out dough into 12-inch circle on lightly floured surface. Transfer to prepared baking sheet. Spread remaining 4 tablespoons barbecue sauce over dough, leaving ½-inch border. Sprinkle with 2 tablespoons mozzarella and 2 tablespoons Gouda. Top with chicken and onion; sprinkle with remaining cheeses.
4. Bake 12 to 15 minutes or until crust is browned and cheese is bubbly. Sprinkle with cilantro. Cut into wedges to serve.

Cubano Burgers

MAKES 4 SERVINGS

- 1½ pounds ground pork
- ¼ cup minced green onions
- 3 tablespoons yellow mustard, divided
- 1 tablespoon minced garlic
- 2 teaspoons paprika
- ½ teaspoon black pepper
- ¼ teaspoon salt
- 8 slices Swiss cheese
- 4 Kaiser rolls or bolillos, split and toasted
- 8 slices sandwich-style dill pickles
- ¼ pound thinly sliced ham

1. Prepare grill for direct cooking over medium heat.
2. Combine pork, green onions, 1 tablespoon mustard, garlic, paprika, pepper and salt in large bowl; mix gently but thoroughly. Shape into four patties about ¾ inch thick, shaping to fit rolls.
3. Grill patties, covered, 8 to 10 minutes (or uncovered, 13 to 15 minutes) or until cooked through (160°F), turning occasionally. Top each burger with 2 slices of Swiss cheese during last 2 minutes of grilling.
4. Spread remaining 2 tablespoons mustard over cut sides of rolls. Place pickles on bottom half of each roll. Top each with burger and ham. Cover with top halves of rolls.

Pesto Turkey Burgers

MAKES 4 SERVINGS

- 1 pound ground turkey
- 2 tablespoons grated onion
- 2 tablespoons pesto sauce, divided
- 2 tablespoons chopped sun-dried tomatoes, divided
- ¼ teaspoon salt
- ¼ teaspoon black pepper
- ¼ cup mayonnaise
- 4 hamburger buns, split
- Lettuce leave, tomato slices and red onion slices

1. Prepare grill for direct cooking over medium heat or preheat broiler. Oil grill grate.
2. Combine turkey, onion, 1 tablespoon pesto sauce, 1 tablespoon sun-dried tomato, salt and pepper in medium bowl; mix well. Shape mixture into four patties about ½ inch thick.
3. Grill or broil patties about 5 minutes per side or until browned and cooked through (165°F).
4. Meanwhile, combine mayonnaise, remaining 1 tablespoon pesto sauce and 1 tablespoon sun-dried tomato in small bowl; mix well.
5. Serve burgers on buns with lettuce, tomato slices, red onion and mayonnaise mixture.

Hamburger-Style Beef Pizza

MAKES 4 TO 6 SERVINGS

- 1 package (about 14 ounces) refrigerated pizza dough
- 8 ounces ground beef
- ½ cup finely chopped onion
- ½ cup finely bell pepper
- ¾ cup pizza sauce
- 1 tomato, peeled, seeded and chopped
- 2 teaspoons Italian seasoning
- 2 cloves garlic, minced
- ¼ teaspoon salt
- ⅛ teaspoon ground red pepper
- ½ cup sliced mushrooms
- 1 cup (4 ounces) shredded mozzarella cheese
- 1 tablespoon grated Parmesan cheese

1. Preheat oven to 425°F. Lightly spray 12-inch pizza pan with nonstick cooking spray. Unroll pizza dough; press onto prepared pan, making slight edge around rim. Poke dough all over with fork. Bake 7 to 10 minutes or until lightly browned.
2. Meanwhile, heat large skillet over medium-high heat. Add beef, onion and bell pepper; cook 6 to 8 minutes or until beef is no longer pink, stirring to break up meat. Drain fat.
3. Combine pizza sauce, tomato, Italian seasoning, garlic, salt and red pepper in small saucepan over medium heat; bring to a boil. Reduce heat; simmer, uncovered, about 8 minutes or until desired consistency.
4. Spread sauce evenly over pizza crust. Top with ground beef mixture and mushrooms; sprinkle with cheeses. Bake 5 to 8 minutes or until cheese is melted. Cut into wedges to serve.

Skillet Suppers

Pepper and Sausage Skillet

MAKES 4 SERVINGS

- 1 pound mild Italian sausage, casings removed
- 1 tablespoon olive oil
- 1 package (8 ounces) sliced mushrooms
- 1 red bell pepper, cut into strips
- 1 green bell pepper, cut into strips
- 1 zucchini, thinly sliced
- ¾ cup finely chopped onion
- 1 tablespoon dried basil
- 1 can (8 ounces) tomato sauce
- ½ cup plain dry bread crumbs
- ¼ teaspoon salt
- 1½ cups (6 ounces) shredded mozzarella cheese

1. Brown sausage in large nonstick skillet over medium-high heat 6 to 8 minutes, stirring to break up meat. Transfer sausage to plate.
2. Heat oil in same skillet over medium-high heat. Add mushrooms, bell peppers, zucchini, onion and basil; cook and stir 5 minutes or until zucchini is tender.
3. Return sausage to skillet. Add tomato sauce, bread crumbs and salt; mix well. Cover and simmer 20 minutes or until bell peppers are tender. Remove from heat. Sprinkle with cheese. Cover; let stand until cheese is melted.

Spiced Chicken and Couscous

MAKES 4 SERVINGS

- ¾ teaspoons ground allspice
- ½ teaspoon ground cinnamon
- ½ teaspoon black pepper
- ¼ teaspoon ground ginger
- ¼ teaspoon ground mustard
- ⅛ teaspoon ground cloves
- ⅛ teaspoon ground red pepper
- ⅛ teaspoon ground coriander
- 1 pound boneless skinless chicken breasts, cut into 1-inch pieces
- ½ teaspoon salt
- 1 tablespoon olive oil
- 1 can (about 14 ounces) chicken broth
- 1 cup uncooked couscous
- ¼ cup golden raisins
- ¼ cup pistachio nuts
- ¼ cup chopped fresh parsley
- 1 teaspoon grated lemon peel

1. Combine allspice, cinnamon, black pepper, ginger, mustard, cloves, red pepper and coriander in small bowl. Sprinkle chicken with 1 teaspoon spice mixture and salt; set remaining spice mixture aside.
2. Heat oil in large nonstick skillet over medium-high heat. Add chicken; cook without stirring 2 minutes or until golden. Turn chicken; cook 2 minutes or until cooked through (165°F) and no longer pink in center.
3. Add broth; bring to a boil. Add couscous and remaining spice mixture; cook 1 minute. Stir in raisins, pistachios, parsley and lemon peel. Remove from heat; cover and let stand 5 minutes. Fluff with fork before serving.

Skillet Lasagna with Vegetables

MAKES 6 SERVINGS

- 8 ounces Italian turkey sausage, casings removed*
- 8 ounces ground turkey*
- ¾ cup chopped yellow or green bell pepper
- 2 stalks celery, sliced
- ⅓ cup chopped onion
- 2 cups marinara sauce
- 1⅓ cups water
- 4 ounces uncooked bowtie pasta (farfalle)
- 1 medium zucchini, halved lengthwise, and cut crosswise into ½-inch slices (2 cups)
- ½ teaspoon salt
- ½ cup (2 ounces) shredded mozzarella cheese
- ½ cup ricotta cheese
- 2 tablespoons finely grated Parmesan cheese
- Chopped fresh parsley

***Or use 1 pound total of ground turkey or sausage.**

1. Heat large skillet over medium-high heat. Add sausage, turkey, bell pepper, celery and onion; cook and stir 6 to 8 minutes or until turkey is no longer pink, stirring to break up meat. Stir in marinara sauce and water; bring to a boil. Stir in pasta, zucchini and salt. Reduce heat to medium-low; cover and simmer 15 minutes or until pasta is al dente. Sprinkle with mozzarella.

2. Combine ricotta cheese and Parmesan cheese in small bowl. Drop by rounded teaspoonfuls on top of lasagna. Remove from heat; cover and let stand 5 minutes. Sprinkle with parsley, if desired.

Cheesy Hamburger Ramen

MAKES 4 SERVINGS

- 1 pound ground beef
- 1 cup chopped red onion
- 1 teaspoon salt, divided
- 2 packages (3 ounces each) ramen noodles*
- 1 tablespoon butter
- 1 tablespoon all-purpose flour
- 1¼ cups milk
- ¼ teaspoon black pepper
- 1 can (about 14 ounces) diced tomatoes, drained
- 1½ cups (6 ounces) shredded sharp Cheddar cheese
- ¼ cup ketchup

***Use any flavor; discard seasoning packets.**

1. Heat large nonstick skillet over medium-high heat. Add beef; cook 4 minutes or just until beginning to brown, stirring to break up meat. Add onion and ½ teaspoon salt; cook and stir 8 minutes or until onion is softened and beef is no longer pink. Transfer to large bowl; keep warm.

2. Meanwhile, bring medium saucepan of water to a boil. Add noodles; cook 3 minutes, stirring frequently to separate noodles. Drain and add to bowl with beef.

3. Melt butter in same skillet over medium heat. Stir in flour; cook and stir 1 minute. Gradually add milk, stirring constantly. Add pepper and remaining ½ teaspoon salt; cook 4 minutes or until mixture is thickened, stirring constantly. Remove from heat. Add tomatoes, cheese and ketchup; stir until cheese is melted. Add sauce to beef mixture; stir until well blended. Serve immediately.

Ham and Swiss Penne Skillet

MAKES 4 SERVINGS

- 8 ounces uncooked penne pasta
- 2 slices sandwich bread, torn into pieces
- 5 tablespoons butter, divided
- 3 tablespoons all-purpose flour
- 2¾ cups milk
- 1 cup thawed frozen corn
- ¾ cup thawed frozen peas
- 6 ounces ham, diced
- 1 cup (4 ounces) shredded Swiss cheese
- ½ cup finely chopped green onions
- Salt and black pepper

1. Cook pasta in large saucepan of salted boiling water according to package directions for al dente. Drain and return to saucepan; keep warm.
2. Place bread in food processor; pulse to form coarse crumbs. Melt 2 tablespoons butter in large skillet over medium heat. Add bread crumbs; cook and stir 2 minutes or until golden. Transfer to plate; set aside.
3. Melt remaining 3 tablespoons butter in same skillet over medium heat. Add flour; whisk 2 minutes or until smooth. Gradually whisk in milk; cook and stir 4 minutes or until slightly thickened.
4. Stir in pasta, corn, peas, ham, cheese and green onions. Season with salt and pepper; cook and stir 4 minutes or until heated through. Sprinkle with bread crumbs. Serve immediately.

Southwestern Tilapia with Rice and Beans

MAKES 4 SERVINGS

- 2 tablespoons all-purpose flour
- ½ teaspoon salt, divided
- ⅛ teaspoon black pepper
- 4 tilapia fillets (about 4 ounces each)
- 2 tablespoons butter, divided
- 1 can (about 15 ounces) black beans, rinsed and drained
- 1 can (about 14 ounces) diced tomatoes with chiles
- 1 package (about 8 ounces) ready-to-serve Spanish rice*
- ¼ teaspoon dried oregano
- 1 green onion, finely chopped

***Or prepare 1 box (about 7 ounces) Spanish rice mix according to package directions.**

1. Combine flour, ¼ teaspoon salt and pepper in shallow bowl; mix well. Coat both sides of fish with flour mixture.
2. Melt 1 tablespoon butter in large skillet over medium-high heat. Add tilapia; cook 2 minutes per side or until golden brown and fish begins to flake when tested with fork. Transfer to plate; tent with foil to keep warm.
3. Melt remaining 1 tablespoon butter in same skillet. Stir in beans, tomatoes, rice, oregano and remaining ¼ teaspoon salt. Reduce heat to low; cook 5 minutes, stirring frequently.
4. Arrange tilapia over rice mixture. Sprinkle with green onion.

Mushroom and Chicken Skillet

MAKES 4 SERVINGS

- 1 pound boneless skinless chicken breasts, cut into bite-size pieces
- 1 can (about 14 ounces) chicken broth
- ¼ cup water
- ½ teaspoon salt
- ½ teaspoon dried thyme
- 2 cups uncooked instant rice
- 1 package (8 ounces) mushrooms, thinly sliced
- 1 can (10½ ounces) condensed cream of celery soup
- Chopped fresh parsley

1. Combine chicken, broth, water, salt and thyme in large nonstick skillet; bring to a boil over high heat. Stir in rice; place mushrooms on top. (Do not stir mushrooms into rice.) Cover skillet; turn off heat and let stand 5 minutes.
2. Stir in condensed soup; cook over low heat 5 minutes or until heated through. Sprinkle with parsley.

Potato and Pork Frittata

MAKES 4 SERVINGS

- 12 ounces (about 3 cups) frozen shredded potatoes or hash browns
- 1 teaspoon Cajun seasoning
- 6 eggs
- ¼ cup milk
- 1 teaspoon dry mustard
- ½ teaspoon salt
- ¼ teaspoon black pepper
- 3 cups frozen stir-fry vegetable blend
- ⅓ cup water
- ¾ cup chopped cooked pork
- ½ cup (2 ounces) shredded Cheddar cheese

1 Preheat oven to 400°F. Spray baking sheet with nonstick cooking spray. Spread potatoes on prepared baking sheet; sprinkle with Cajun seasoning. Bake 15 minutes or until hot. Remove from oven. *Reduce oven temperature to 350°F.*

2 Meanwhile, beat eggs, milk, mustard, salt and pepper in medium bowl until well blended. Combine vegetables and water in medium ovenproof nonstick skillet; cook over medium heat 5 minutes or until vegetables are crisp-tender; drain. Add potatoes and pork to vegetables in skillet; stir gently. Pour egg mixture evenly over all; sprinkle with cheese. Cook over medium-low heat 5 minutes.

3 Bake 5 minutes or until egg mixture is set and cheese is melted. Cut into wedges to serve.

Chicken and Red Peppers with Parmesan Penne

MAKES 4 SERVINGS

- 8 ounces uncooked penne pasta
- 2 tablespoons olive oil, divided
- 4 boneless skinless chicken breasts (about 6 ounces each)
- 1 medium onion, chopped
- 2 teaspoons minced garlic
- 1 tablespoon flour
- ½ cup chicken broth
- 1 jar (about 12 ounces) roasted red bell peppers, drained and chopped
- ¾ cup grated Parmesan cheese, divided
- ¼ cup half-and-half
- ½ teaspoon salt
- ½ teaspoon black pepper

1. Cook pasta in large saucepan of salted boiling water according to package directions for al dente. Drain and return to saucepan; keep warm.
2. Meanwhile, heat 1 tablespoon oil in large skillet over medium-high heat. Brown chicken on both sides. Cover and cook 15 minutes or until cooked through (165°F) and no longer pink in center, turning once. Transfer to plate; cover and keep warm.
3. Heat remaining 1 tablespoon oil in same skillet over medium heat. Add onion; cook and stir 3 minutes or until translucent. Add garlic; cook 1 minute. Add flour; stir until smooth. Add broth; cook and stir until slightly thickened. Stir in pasta, bell peppers, ½ cup Parmesan cheese, half-and-half, salt and black pepper.
4. Top with chicken; cover and simmer 5 to 10 minutes or until heated through. Sprinkle with remaining ¼ cup Parmesan cheese. Serve immediately.

Tomato and Potato Skillet

MAKES 4 SERVINGS

- 1 tablespoon olive oil, divided
- 2 cups thinly sliced potatoes
- ⅓ cup minced fresh basil
- 4 eggs
- 2 tablespoons milk
- 1 tablespoon Dijon mustard
- 1 teaspoon dry mustard
- ½ teaspoon salt
- ¼ teaspoon black pepper
- 2 plum tomatoes, sliced

1 Heat oil in medium nonstick skillet over medium heat. Add potatoes; cover and cook 5 minutes or until lightly browned. Turn potatoes; cover and cook 5 minutes or until lightly browned.

2 Spread potatoes in single layer in skillet. Sprinkle with basil. Whisk eggs, milk, mustards, salt and pepper in small bowl. Pour over potatoes; top with tomatoes. Reduce heat to low; cover and cook 10 minutes or until eggs are set. Cut into wedges to serve.

Chicken Couscous

MAKES 4 SERVINGS

- 1 tablespoon olive oil
- 1 pound boneless skinless chicken breasts, cut into 1-inch cubes
- 1 teaspoon salt
- 4 medium zucchini, sliced
- 1 can (about 14 ounces) diced tomatoes
- 1 can (about 14 ounces) chicken broth
- 1 teaspoon Italian seasoning
- 1 cup uncooked couscous

1. Heat oil in large skillet over medium-high heat. Add chicken and sprinkle with salt; cook and stir 4 minutes or until lightly browned.
2. Add zucchini, tomatoes, broth and Italian seasoning. Reduce heat to low; simmer 15 minutes, stirring occasionally.
3. Stir in couscous; remove from heat. Cover and let stand 7 minutes. Fluff with fork.

Mexican Skillet Casserole

MAKES 4 SERVINGS

- 1 tablespoon vegetable oil
- 1 pound ground turkey
- 1 can (about 14 ounces) diced tomatoes
- ½ (16-ounce) package frozen bell pepper stir-fry blend, thawed
- ¾ teaspoon ground cumin
- ½ teaspoon salt
- ½ cup (2 ounces) finely shredded sharp Cheddar cheese
- 2 ounces tortilla chips, lightly crushed

1. Heat oil in large cast iron skillet over medium heat. Add turkey; cook 6 to 8 minutes or until no longer pink, stirring to break up meat. Stir in tomatoes, bell peppers, cumin and salt; bring to a boil. Reduce heat to low; cover and simmer 20 minutes or until vegetables are tender.
2. Sprinkle evenly with cheese and chips; let stand until cheese is melted.

Steak Fajitas

MAKES 2 SERVINGS

- 2 tablespoons lime juice
- 2 tablespoons soy sauce
- 3 tablespoons vegetable oil, divided
- 1 tablespoon honey
- 1 tablespoon Worcestershire sauce
- 2 cloves garlic, minced
- ½ teaspoon ground red pepper
- 1 pound flank steak, skirt steak or top sirloin
- Salt and black pepper
- 1 small yellow onion, halved and cut into ½-inch slices
- 1 small red onion, halved and cut into ½-inch slices
- 1 *each* small red, yellow and green bell pepper, sliced
- Flour tortillas, warmed
- Optional toppings: pico de gallo, guacamole, sour cream, shredded lettuce and shredded Cheddar-Jack cheese

1 Whisk lime juice, soy sauce, 1 tablespoon oil, honey, Worcestershire sauce, garlic and ground red pepper in medium bowl. Season steak all over with salt and black pepper.

2 Heat 1 tablespoon oil in large grill pan over medium-high heat. Add steak; cook 4 minutes. Turn and cook 4 minutes for medium rare or to desired doneness. Pour in half of lime juice mixture; cook about 30 seconds or until steak is glazed, turning once to coat. Remove to cutting board; tent with foil and let stand 10 minutes.

3 Meanwhile, wipe out grill pan. Heat remaining 1 tablespoon oil in grill pan over medium-high heat. Add onions and bell peppers; cook 8 minutes or until vegetables are crisp-tender and beginning to brown in spots, stirring occasionally. (Cook in two batches if necessary; do not crowd vegetables in skillet.) Add remaining lime juice mixture; cook and stir 30 seconds or until glazed.

4 Cut steak into thin slices across the grain. Serve with vegetables, tortillas, lime wedges and desired toppings.

Salsa Shrimp and Rice

MAKES 4 SERVINGS

- 1 cup uncooked rice
- 1 tablespoon olive oil
- ½ cup chopped onion
- 1 clove garlic, minced
- 1 cup salsa verde
- ¾ cup dry white wine
- 1 tablespoon lemon juice
- 12 ounces medium raw shrimp, peeled (with tails on)

1 Cook rice according to package directions; keep warm.

2 Meanwhile, heat oil in large nonstick skillet over medium-high heat. Add onion; cook and stir 3 minutes or until onion is translucent. Add garlic; cook and stir 1 minute. Add salsa, wine and lemon juice; bring to a boil. Reduce heat to medium-low; simmer 10 minutes.

3 Add shrimp; cook about 2 minutes or until shrimp turn pink and opaque, stirring occasionally. Serve shrimp mixture over rice.

Bratwurst Skillet

MAKES 4 SERVINGS

- 1 pound bratwurst, cut into ½-inch slices
- 1½ cups sliced onions
- 1 green bell pepper, thinly sliced
- 1 red bell pepper, thinly sliced
- 1 teaspoon paprika
- 1 teaspoon caraway seeds
- Salt and black pepper

1 Heat large skillet over medium heat. Add bratwurst; cover and cook about 5 minutes or until browned and no longer pink in center. Transfer bratwurst to bowl; cover and keep warm.

2 Drain all but 1 tablespoon drippings from skillet. Add onions, bell peppers, paprika and caraway seeds; cook and stir about 5 minutes or until vegetables are tender. Season to taste with salt and black pepper. Return bratwurst to skillet; mix well.

Speedy Sides

Cinnamon Apples

MAKES 4 SERVINGS

- **¼ cup (½ stick) butter**
- **3 tart red apples such as Gala, Fuji or Honeycrisp (about 1½ pounds total), peeled and cut into ½-inch wedges**
- **¼ cup packed brown sugar**
- **1 teaspoon ground cinnamon**
- **⅛ teaspoon ground nutmeg**
- **⅛ teaspoon salt**
- **1 tablespoon cornstarch**

1. Melt butter in large skillet over medium-high heat. Add apples; cook 8 minutes or until tender, stirring occasionally.
2. Add brown sugar, cinnamon, nutmeg and salt; cook and stir 1 minute or until apples are glazed. Reduce heat to medium-low; stir in cornstarch until well blended.
3. Remove from heat; let stand 5 minutes for glaze to thicken. Stir again; serve immediately.

Brussels Sprouts with Honey Butter

MAKES 4 SERVINGS

- 6 slices thick-cut bacon, cut into ½-inch pieces
- 1½ pounds Brussels sprouts (about 24 medium), halved
- ¼ teaspoon salt
- ¼ teaspoon black pepper
- 2 tablespoons butter, softened
- 2 tablespoons honey

1. Preheat oven to 400°F. Cook bacon in medium skillet until almost crisp. Drain on paper towel-lined plate. Reserve 1 tablespoon drippings.
2. Place Brussels sprouts on large baking sheet. Drizzle with reserved bacon drippings and sprinkle with salt and pepper; toss to coat. Arrange Brussels sprouts cut sides down in single layer on baking sheet.
3. Roast 20 to 25 minutes or until Brussels sprouts are browned, stirring once.
4. Whisk butter and honey in medium bowl until well blended. Add roasted Brussels sprouts; stir until completely coated. Stir in bacon; season to taste with additional salt and pepper.

Crunchy Kale Salad

MAKES 6 SERVINGS

- ¼ cup cider vinegar
- ¼ cup extra virgin olive oil
- ¼ cup maple syrup
- 1 tablespoon lemon juice
- ½ tablespoon Dijon mustard
- ½ teaspoon salt
- ¼ teaspoon black pepper
- 10 cups chopped stemmed kale (about 1 large bunch)
- 2 cups shredded green cabbage
- ½ cup sliced almonds, toasted*

**To toast almonds, spread in small skillet. Cook and stir over medium-low heat 2 to 3 minutes or until fragrant.*

1. Whisk vinegar, oil, maple syrup, lemon juice, mustard, salt and pepper in small bowl or measuring cup until well blended.
2. Combine kale and cabbage in large bowl. Pour dressing over vegetables; massage kale with hands 3 to 4 minutes to soften.
3. Stir in almonds just before serving.

Broccoli and Cheese

MAKES 4 TO 6 SERVINGS

- **2 medium crowns broccoli (1½ pounds), cut into florets (about 6½ cups)**
- **2 tablespoons butter**
- **2 tablespoons all-purpose flour**
- **1½ cups milk**
- **½ teaspoon salt**
- **⅛ teaspoon ground nutmeg**
- **⅛ teaspoon ground red pepper**
- **1 cup (4 ounces) shredded Cheddar cheese**
- **½ cup (2 ounces) shredded Monterey Jack cheese**
- **¼ cup shredded Parmesan cheese**
- **Paprika (optional)**

1. Bring large saucepan of water to a boil over medium-high heat. Add broccoli; cook 5 minutes or until tender.
2. Meanwhile, melt butter in medium saucepan over medium-high heat. Add flour; whisk until smooth. Gradually whisk in milk until well blended. Cook 2 minutes or until thickened, whisking frequently. Stir in salt, nutmeg and red pepper. Reduce heat to low; whisk in cheeses in three additions, whisking well after first two additions and stirring just until blended after last addition.
3. Drain broccoli; place on serving plates. Top with cheese sauce; garnish with paprika. Serve immediately.

Wedge Salad

MAKES 4 SERVINGS

Dressing

¾ cup mayonnaise
½ cup buttermilk
1 cup crumbled blue cheese, divided
1 clove garlic, minced
½ teaspoon sugar
⅛ teaspoon onion powder
⅛ teaspoon salt
⅛ teaspoon black pepper

Salad

1 head iceberg lettuce
1 large tomato, diced (about 1 cup)
½ small red onion, cut into thin rings
½ cup crumbled crisp-cooked bacon (6 to 8 slices)

1 For dressing, combine mayonnaise, buttermilk, ½ cup cheese, garlic, sugar, onion powder, salt and pepper in food processor or blender; process until smooth.

2 For salad, cut lettuce into quarters through stem end; remove stem from each wedge.

3 Place lettuce wedges on individual serving plates; top with dressing. Sprinkle with tomato, onion, remaining ½ cup cheese and bacon.

Smashed Potatoes

MAKES 4 SERVINGS

- 4 medium russet potatoes (about 1½ pounds), peeled and cut into ¼-inch pieces
- ⅓ cup milk
- 2 tablespoons sour cream
- 1 tablespoon minced onion
- ½ teaspoon salt
- ¼ teaspoon black pepper
- ⅛ teaspoon garlic powder (optional)
- Chopped fresh chives or French fried onions (optional)

1 Bring large saucepan of lightly salted water to a boil over medium-high heat. Add potatoes; cook 15 to 20 minutes or until fork-tender. Drain and return to saucepan.

2 Slightly mash potatoes. Stir in milk, sour cream, minced onion, salt, pepper and garlic powder, if desired; mash until desired texture is reached, leaving potatoes chunky. Cook 5 minutes over low heat or until heated through, stirring occasionally. Garnish with chives.

Mediterranean Orzo and Vegetable Pilaf

MAKES 6 SERVINGS

- 4 ounces (½ cup plus 2 tablespoons) uncooked orzo pasta
- 2 teaspoons olive oil
- 1 small onion, diced
- 2 cloves garlic, minced
- 1 small zucchini, diced
- ½ cup vegetable broth
- 1 can (about 14 ounces) artichoke hearts, drained and quartered
- 1 medium tomato, chopped
- ½ teaspoon dried oregano
- ½ teaspoon salt
- ¼ teaspoon black pepper
- ½ cup crumbled feta cheese
- Sliced black olives (optional)

1. Cook orzo in large saucepan of salted boiling water according to package directions for al dente. Drain.

2. Meanwhile, heat oil in large skillet over medium heat. Add onion; cook and stir 5 minutes or until translucent. Add garlic; cook and stir 1 minute. Reduce heat to low. Stir in zucchini and broth; cook 5 minutes or until zucchini is crisp-tender.

3. Add orzo, artichokes, tomato, oregano, salt and pepper; cook and stir 1 minute or until heated through. Top with cheese and olives, if desired.

Black Beans with Bacon and Poblano Peppers

MAKES 4 SERVINGS

- 2 slices bacon
- 2 medium poblano peppers, seeded and chopped
- 1 small onion, chopped
- 2 cloves garlic, minced
- 1 teaspoon salt, divided
- ½ teaspoon chili powder
- 1 can (about 15 ounces) black beans, rinsed and drained
- ⅓ cup water

1 Cook bacon in large skillet over medium-high heat 6 to 7 minutes or until crisp, turning occasionally. Drain on paper towel-lined plate. Chop bacon; set aside.

2 Add poblanos, onion, garlic, ½ teaspoon salt and chili powder to same skillet; cook and stir 5 minutes or until crisp-tender. Add beans, water and remaining ½ teaspoon salt; cook 10 minutes or until liquid is absorbed and vegetables are tender, stirring occasionally.

3 Stir in bacon just before serving.

Spinach and Couscous Salad

MAKES 4 SERVINGS

- 1 cup water
- ¾ cup uncooked couscous
- ½ teaspoon salt
- ½ (15-ounce) can white beans, rinsed and drained
- 1 cup packed spinach, coarsely chopped
- 1 can (2¼ ounces) sliced black olives, drained
- 3 slices (1 ounce) hard salami, cut into thin strips
- 3 tablespoons vinaigrette
- 3 tablespoons cider vinegar
- 1 tablespoon dried oregano
- 1½ teaspoons dried basil
- ⅛ teaspoon red pepper flakes
- 3 ounces crumbled sun-dried tomato and basil feta cheese

1 Bring water to a boil in small saucepan over high heat. Stir in couscous and salt. Remove from heat; cover and let stand 5 minutes or until liquid is absorbed. Transfer couscous to large bowl; cool slightly, fluffing with fork occasionally.

2 Add beans, spinach, olives, salami, vinaigrette, vinegar, oregano, basil and red pepper flakes to couscous; mix well. Add cheese; toss gently.

Greek-Style Cucumber Salad

MAKES 4 SERVINGS

- 1 medium cucumber, peeled and diced
- ¼ cup chopped green onions
- 1 teaspoon minced fresh dill
- 1 clove garlic, minced
- 1 cup sour cream
- ½ teaspoon salt
- ¼ teaspoon black pepper
- ⅛ teaspoon ground cumin
- Lemon juice (optional)

1. Combine cucumber, green onions, dill and garlic in medium bowl.
2. Combine sour cream, salt, pepper and cumin in small bowl; stir until blended. Add to cucumber mixture; mix well. Sprinkle with lemon juice to taste, if desired.

Bulgur Pilaf with Caramelized Onions and Kale

MAKES 4 SERVINGS

- 1 tablespoon olive oil
- 1 small onion, cut into thin wedges
- 1 clove garlic, minced
- 2 cups chopped kale
- 2 cups vegetable broth
- ¾ cup medium grain bulgur
- ½ teaspoon salt
- ¼ teaspoon black pepper

1 Heat oil in large skillet over medium heat. Add onion; cook 8 minutes or until softened and lightly browned, stirring frequently. Add garlic; cook and stir 1 minute. Add kale; cook and stir about 1 minute or until kale is wilted.

2 Stir in broth, bulgur, salt and pepper; bring to a boil. Reduce heat to low; cover and simmer 12 minutes or until liquid is absorbed and bulgur is tender.

Index

Index

Index

Index

T

U

V

W

Z

Metric Conversion Chart

VOLUME MEASUREMENTS (dry)

1/8 teaspoon = 0.5 mL
1/4 teaspoon = 1 mL
1/2 teaspoon = 2 mL
3/4 teaspoon = 4 mL
1 teaspoon = 5 mL
1 tablespoon = 15 mL
2 tablespoons = 30 mL
1/4 cup = 60 mL
1/3 cup = 75 mL
1/2 cup = 125 mL
2/3 cup = 150 mL
3/4 cup = 175 mL
1 cup = 250 mL
2 cups = 1 pint = 500 mL
3 cups = 750 mL
4 cups = 1 quart = 1 L

VOLUME MEASUREMENTS (fluid)

1 fluid ounce (2 tablespoons) = 30 mL
4 fluid ounces (1/2 cup) = 125 mL
8 fluid ounces (1 cup) = 250 mL
12 fluid ounces (1 1/2 cups) = 375 mL
16 fluid ounces (2 cups) = 500 mL

WEIGHTS (mass)

1/2 ounce = 15 g
1 ounce = 30 g
3 ounces = 90 g
4 ounces = 120 g
8 ounces = 225 g
10 ounces = 285 g
12 ounces = 360 g
16 ounces = 1 pound = 450 g

DIMENSIONS

1/16 inch = 2 mm
1/8 inch = 3 mm
1/4 inch = 6 mm
1/2 inch = 1.5 cm
3/4 inch = 2 cm
1 inch = 2.5 cm

OVEN TEMPERATURES

250°F = 120°C
275°F = 140°C
300°F = 150°C
325°F = 160°C
350°F = 180°C
375°F = 190°C
400°F = 200°C
425°F = 220°C
450°F = 230°C

BAKING PAN SIZES

Utensil	Size in Inches/Quarts	Metric Volume	Size in Centimeters
Baking or Cake Pan (square or rectangular)	8×8×2	2 L	20×20×5
	9×9×2	2.5 L	23×23×5
	12×8×2	3 L	30×20×5
	13×9×2	3.5 L	33×23×5
Loaf Pan	8×4×3	1.5 L	20×10×7
	9×5×3	2 L	23×13×7
Round Layer Cake Pan	8×1½	1.2 L	20×4
	9×1½	1.5 L	23×4
Pie Plate	8×1¼	750 mL	20×3
	9×1¼	1 L	23×3
Baking Dish or Casserole	1 quart	1 L	—
	1½ quart	1.5 L	—
	2 quart	2 L	—